Remembering Blue

Colin Bell

Published by Ward Wood Publishing
6 The Drive
Golders Green
London NW11 9SR
www.wardwoodpublishing.co.uk

The right of Colin Bell to be identified as author of this work has been asserted by him in accordance with the Copyright, Designs and Patent Act, 1988.
Copyright © 2019 Colin Bell
ISBN: 978-1-908742-70-4

British Library Cataloguing in Publication Data. A CIP record for this book can be obtained from the British Library.

All rights reserved. No part of this publication may be reproduced, stored in a retrieval system, or transmitted in any form or by any means, electronic, mechanical, photocopying, recording or otherwise without the prior written permission of the publishers. This book may not be lent, hired out, resold or otherwise disposed of by way of trade in any form of binding or cover other than that in which it is published, without the prior consent of the publishers.

Designed and typeset in Palatino Linotype by
Ward Wood Publishing.
Cover design and artwork by Kayla Bell
Copyright © 2019 Kayla Bell.

Printed and bound in Great Britain by
Imprint Digital, Seychelles Farm,
Upton Pyne, Exeter, Devon EX5 5HY

Contents

Haiku	7
Four-Minute Song	8
Ten-Finger Exercise	9
Home Movie	10
Razor-Sharp	11
The Tale of an Apple and a Sausage	13
High-Flyer	14
The Sea Says	15
Naked Man	16
Wrestling Angels	17
Strangers on a Train	18
The Great Escape	19
So Civilised	20
On Thursday	22
Escaping	23
Society Contracts	24
A Step Away from Frank	26
The Imperial Stamp	28
Kneeling	29
Outside the Cathedral	30
Basque	32
Miss Prism's Handbag	33
Nude Ascending a Staircase	35
Mind the Gap	37
Crouching Tigers	38
Aleppo	40
Waiting	41
Sicilian Vespas	42
Butterfly	44
Mollusc	46
The Battle of Princeton	47
Hummingbird Feeder	48
The Blueberry Cage	49
Desert Nights	50
Dido in Carthage	51
The Awakening	52

Looking for Fernando Pessoa	53
The Odalisque	54
Rosarium	
1. Falstaff	55
2. Golden Celebration	55
3. Danse de Feu	56
4. Iceberg	56
5. Benjamin Britten	57
Gardening Tip	58
Lewes Castle	59
In Kiln Wood	60
November Landscape	61
Waterlogged	62
Postcards	63
Sète	64
Mortwick Village	65
The Storm Brewed	66
Ansel	67
Sortie	68
Eve	69
Proffer Your Hand	70
Entanglement	71
Time Travels	72
My Seat in the Quire	73
At the Crossroads	75
October 30th 2008	76
In Extremis	80

Notes	81
Acknowledgements	84
About the Author	85

*For my parents
Andy and Irene Bell*

Haiku

This blank page is grey
I shall write rain and cloud here
but remember blue.

Four-Minute Song
After Robert Lowell

Furniture auctioned, old letters boxed –
why are they no help to me now?
A father's photography – tricycle days,
landscapes once playgrounds,
small hands held by ghosts.
Why no help those four-minute songs
– The Beatles' raw anthems of hope?
Rachmaninov's G minor tragedy
no longer brings a tear.
The Russian's melancholy fitted me once
like the thrill of Gauloises cigarettes.
Moving away from familiar rooms,
time to write my own four-minute song,
to sing unaccompanied this time.

Ten-Finger Exercise

I've always spelt words on my fingers,
it's the way I talk to myself.
At first it was checking the spelling
but then certain words became special –
those that fitted on all ten digits,
two handfuls of consonants and vowels.
Achievement, I found, is one letter too long,
Success three too short.
Friendship is cosily perfect with every finger flexed;
Loneliness less alone as a *comforting* ten-letter word.

I find power in phrases and sentences
that make a neat fit on both hands.
It's an obsessive's pleasure in precision.
This is good, I think, counting to ten.
We have found a way of talking,
me and my *finger-songs.*
You can do it... they sing *when I'm nervous*
Yes, yes, I can... I type back.
My fingers are silent cheerleaders.
I need their help to go on.

Some words and phrases sound warnings:
I love you is two fingers short.
Happiness misses by one
but *Frightened* makes ten and feels like a hug –
it's somewhere to *bury my head.*
Hands and brain unite to chant mantras
like a pianist practising scales.
Repeat them, repeat them, repeat them.
I beat out these rhythms and, by counting,
keep every day finger-controlled.

Home Movie
for Graham Bell

Flickering monochrome from another time:
two small boys at a five-bar gate.
Movie-making on a winter's day:
brothers waving goodbye.

The six-year-old is the star of the show –
centre of attention,
master of the universe,
confidently centre screen.

The four-year-old is the witness.
Not there for the record, not there to be seen,
his inner camera is rolling.

We look at each other, me and me,
separated by all those years.
Our eyes meet in recognition,
something forgotten revealed.

Don't get it wrong, the little boy says
with a shyly knowing squint.
You know I know who you are,
do you remember me?

Razor-Sharp

Wiry enough to climb through a back window,
he'd come to the door wheeling his bike.
Not shy to thunder the gargoyled knocker
frightening the boy alone in the house.

Any knives you want sharpening?
I'll make your blades razor-sharp.

The boy dwarfed in the doorway says nothing –
curious, staring, not thinking he can be seen.

Oily hands indigo under the nails –
calluses highlighted, sooty mascara.
Cloth cap, tweed jacket, work-impregnated,
labourer's boots unpolished by dust.

The boy is bewitched by the Victorian bike –
a magic machine from a storybook past.
Here, let me show you – out comes the knife,
bone-handled, thrilling, an assassin's stiletto.

Wheels linked to chains linked to pulleys and belts,
all motion harnessed, the bike clamped to the path,
pedalling nowhere, the grindstone rotated.
A real man's work, sparks, noise and smoke.

No oil on the boy's shiny red trike –
there on the grass, all gloss paint and chrome.
Fun usually comes here in primary colours.
Plastic grenadier guards line up in the hall.

So, what have you got?
Scissors? Axes? Your dad's bayonet?

The old carving knife in a forbidden drawer.
Sunday-roast-blunted, rapier steel.
The blade-sharpener smiles – hints of gold teeth
– the boy grins too, proud, presenting his weapon.

These make good cutters. Anything else?

The Tale of an Apple and a Sausage

My dog stole the sausage
He knew it was wrong
No, he knew I was cross
Well, he knew I could hurt him
He ate it anyway

I ate the apple
They gave it to me,
the naked couple, man and wife
They got it from a snake
who knew just what they were like

They knew it was wrong
No, they knew there'd be trouble
They ate it anyway
They felt the punishment
and so do we

They got chucked out
They lost out
God's pets
at play in the garden,
free from knowledge, understanding and pain

I ate that apple
It was OK,
juicy in parts with a bitter core
Not what you expect
but no point in spitting it out

High-Flyer

Small rat with big brown eyes,
up above the world so high,
why so surprised on the ride of your life?

Did you never dream of upward propulsion
or imagine the rush of aerodynamics?

Fluffily plump, puffed up and rounded,
speed away from us here, a creature of air,
thrilled or unnerved, your little feet dangling.

A Walt Disney rodent, so cute, almost cuddly,
suspended up there in the bald eagle's grip.

Scampering earthbound did you never look up?
Did no one tell you there are powers above?
They snatch us away without warning.

The Sea Says

The sea says remember me, I showed you how to drown,
teaching you rejection in my waves' embrace.
Those body shocks, the terror, were your birthing pains.
You battled for breath, lungs filled with rage,
when I took your merman's tail.

I washed you up, threw you back –
you – crumpled on the shore.
Choking for rebirth, bloodied on the rocks,
you stood, fist-toed, granite-grazed.
Asphyxiated fish died at your feet.

I'm your paramour on golden days, I hold you in my arms,
whispering warm-breathed promises I can never keep:
Float free, shed your fear, embrace the day, be calmed.
I muffle earthly pains for you and let you drift caressed,
speaking of eternity, all bodies joined with mine.

You know I lie, I'm not your friend –
it was you who invented my smiling face.
Walk the shores, enjoy the views, let sweet water lull you.
My tide will turn, you know that too,
I prepared you for this.

Naked Man
for Allen Ginsberg and Peter Orlovsky

It was a fourth-floor apartment on the Lower East Side,
fire-escapes to the street, New York style,
sulphur fumes and grimy brick,
tenements dressed in steel.

Inside, up there, the literary Buddhist,
incense, chimes and books,
inhaled serenity, lotus-positioned,
a world apart from below.

Then, at the window, the naked man,
with a victory grin that soon fades.
Not wanted, he sees, he knew it before,
but too high now to turn and go down.

An old romance reduced:
the sad, anguished face of the poet-priest,
and the crazed, desperate, naked man
holding their past on a frayed climbing-rope.

Don't jump,
don't howl,
accept the pain.
It often ends like this.

Wrestling Angels

I was bored, restless, but friends said I wasn't drunk;
later that was, when I saw them – afterwards of course.
She might have been an angel but I don't remember her;
there was a party, flamenco dancing on a wooden floor.

She'd saved me, so they said, from an orgy in Gomorrah;
I'd been seen in a taxi with someone dressed in white.
Continuing the fun, I heard, but no one saw her face.
I don't remember this – just flamenco and red wine.

I thought she was an angel; it was that letter on the mat:
I used it in the morning to find out where I was.
It was addressed to Anne Angel – a coincidence perhaps –
on a street in Angel Islington – I'd not been there before.

I don't know much of angels but they frighten me.
God's messengers, avengers, spirits who prophesy.
I preferred those dancing girls who gave me castanets,
and memories of good times in late night Spanish bars.

I woke alone next morning on a stranger's crumpled bed
feeling I'd been wicked but not knowing what I'd done.
My malaise, more than an after-taste of cigarettes and wine,
was, I thought, a warning with no words attached.

She'd gone to more ethereal climes and my clothes lay on
    the floor;
the pockets bulged with feathers, gaudily pink and bright.
I was a fallen fighter left lying on my back
glimpsing distant thrills but nursing aching thighs.

Strangers on a Train

Never look drunks in the eye,
said the man with the broken nose.
I was on a Friday night train, long distance,
half-reading a book when I noticed

that glint in the eye of the hunter.
It persisted, zoom-lensed, camouflaged.
I could have smiled though I didn't, but
my face sometimes smiles without me.

The carriage emptied at a darkened station;
the passengers, raincoated, rushed home.
Alone, perplexed, surprised by sadness,
I saw something by my foot on the floor.

A crumpled page torn from a diary,
scribbled words and a row of digits,
the black spider scrawling a mystery.
An adventure promised then thwarted.

It was probably litter, a redundant list
discarded that night going North,
but I saw my face in the window
and there it was – my smile.

The Great Escape
for Stui

In that desk, some ornaments,
an art deco bowl and a photo frame,
stored away from parental eyes,
buried treasure for another time.

Cake pillars and bone china mugs,
a soap dispenser – random things,
entries on a secret list
quietly intoned as a mantra.

Prayers are whispered every night,
escapist dreams repeated
from a single bed in a barren room,
a hermit's febrile vision.

Tea towels, with rural scenes,
a single, long-stemmed crystal glass,
all packed, ready, hidden.
Left behind when you dared to run.

So Civilised

Your coffee is Fairtrade Yirgacheffe,
sipped from a *Free Tibet* mug.
You thumb your way – so grimly today –
through dog-eared magazines on the sofa.

A lava-shell massage in Gwent could be fun;
Swedish yoga, out of season, how nice;
bath-robed in Borntrorpet;
oiled in Skinnskatteberg.

Single ticket returns, folk rock, nothing heavy.
Yes, *Mumford and Sons* in Chelmsford.
That Shoreditch photographers' gallery looks good
– so rude Warhol's nudiest nudes.

Your wine club sends Burgundy bin-ends
– they're not from that friend in Auxerre.
What happened to him, pas pour toujours,
ton amour? Jean-Phillipe and your last pied-à-terre.

You cycle to Camden for black Kalamon olives,
to St Pancras for Anatolian pastrami – must-haves.
While lovelorn Irena, the au pair from Slovenia
bakes ciabatta, Mlin Katić, in the Aga.

Botoxed.
Detoxed.
Trendy socks.

An unopened *Amnesty* package
still lies on the mat in the hall.
That *Greenpeace* badge went off to Oxfam
on last winter's, last season's, duffle coat.

Organic.
Colonic.
Ironic.

So civilised, so Sondheim, so depressed.
Go on, give your therapist a rest.

On Thursday
for Richard Oakley

White petrified roses stare, frost-embalmed,
lingering passion fruits, a forgotten harvest,
the nasturtiums have blackened in the night.
It was similar to this
on Thursday.

Thick socks pulled up under draughty denim,
belt buckled on the first hole,
black sheep's wool sweater hanging loose.
It seemed suitable
on Thursday.

He'd already gone when the news came in,
draped with sorrow and wrapped in a shroud.
A second passing – a silence felt.
It was something like this
on Thursday.

Escaping

The warrior spot-lit by lampposts,
a one-man minimalist revolt.
Loiter here on a street corner,
chewing gum, hands in pockets, lip curled.
Pass the time, rehearse the look.
Kick a can and shimmy away,
key-scraping the railings.
Heroic enough, this rebellion.

Break the silence.
Disturb the peace.
Your iPod has made you a star.

You're choreographed by drumbeats,
the prowling king of the street,
selecting shadow-cloaked strangers
to join you up there in your head.
Ignore shop window reflections,
you're not just a kid in a hoodie.
Tonight, you have dangerous powers –
reborn in a guitar riff.

Society Contracts

All men are born equal: it's difficult to be equal on the playing field.

People shared out their work to make society. Some became hunters, others, farmers or minstrels. A few people became murderers.

All men are born equal: it's easier to shout it than to live it.

1. It is forbidden for anyone without a certificate of exemption to leave their homes between 22.00 hours and 07.00 hours.

Equal in Slough. Equal at Eton.

Enoch Powell said all political careers end in failure.

One for you.
Two for him.
A lot more for me.

A murderer was like a hunter but less useful.

2. Each player must write down definitions on sheets of paper attached to the other players' backs.

Votes for women.
One man, one vote.
Equal at the ballot box.

Margaret Thatcher left office in tears. At her funeral, politicians looked sad, thinking of Enoch Powell.

3. Everyone must wear an authorised uniform.

4. Meals must be consumed in designated eating areas.

No taxation without representation.
No taxation if your bank is off-shore.

5. Children can sleep with blankets over their heads.

6. All the other players close their eyes and count to one hundred.

It was possible to avoid being murdered by lying very still.

7. The answer will be hidden until the end of the game.

A Step Away from Frank
for Frank O'Hara on Joni Mitchell's 70th Birthday

Manhattan walking, a lunchtime indulgence
destination-free.
Thinking about songs,
my friends *New World*-born.

Hum-coloured cab-watching
on steam-grilled sidewalks
Strolling down Broadway,
still noon-enraptured.

Looking out for the labourers
up there, sky high, washing windows.
Wanting their bravery,
wanting to protect them.

Rising upwards,
flipping over myself,
my feet fly above my head
and higher.

A working lunch, TV days –
Peter Orlovsky nude on a ladder.
Cream in my coffee, cream cheese bagels,
Allen Ginsberg's affectionate finger.

Postprandial in the Lone Star Café.
The man from *The Byrds*, 'Jim' McGuinn
talking and smiling, misty grey portraits,
Beatles, Beachboys and the Tambourine Man.

Delight. The midday light.
The cityscape sings
forgotten encounters re-encountered,
soft-shoe shuffling radio days.

Joni Mitchell there at my back
drawing me home to all the others,
the lost and the living
all there in the garden.

Frank O'Hara in my pocket,
perfect lunch date.
You and me. We are there too.
Our lost halves found.

The Imperial Stamp

There's power in the moment of stamping.
Documents created in unknown lands
authorised here with the imperial seal
by a musicianly white-skinned hand.

Her Majesty's officer, in tropical suit,
sits under the whirl of a ceiling-fan.
Each dull thud, an authorisation,
for ocean-bound ships from unknown lands.

Sitting numbed in an office, palm tree shadowed,
he beckons the World to send its goods.
Boxes from Trinidad, Nairobi, Port Arthur
– the fruits of labourers he'll never meet.

This time a grand piano from Leipzig,
tea in chests from Tanganyika,
ball gowns, Paris' latest, six months late.
The stamp grants permission – *in loco Regina*.

Then the memory returns – a watery mountain,
prayers below deck tasting of bile.
Thy will be done, O monstrous Poseidon.
Anglican gods hide in home county churches.

Never a sailor-lad, this porcelain man
– sun bleached hair, a sickly face.
His only voyage that outward journey
– one-way ticket to an Imperial grave.

He knows the secrets in each landed crate
placed here, with respect, at his feet, on the docks.
His interest severed with a tick on a clipboard
– documented, dispatched, duty done.

Kneeling

On our knees
raised to a knighthood.

On our knees
humiliated.

On our knees
decapitated.

On our knees
manipulated,

eyes closed, incense drunk,
we mumble Amen.

Outside the Cathedral

Santa Maria Maggiore,
beautiful words for foreigners.
Saint Mary the Greater,
in English it sounds C of E.
Santa Maria Maggiore,
whisper it, *sotto voce,*
under the breath: *Santa Maria,*
prega per noi peccatori.
Italian words seduce us
to a world beyond the mundane.

Santa Maria Maggiore,
Grey-domed, pigeon-fluttered,
a sanctuary in the centre of Rome.
Basso profundo bells
punch the solar plexus
calling the faithful to Mass.
Open to all who dare:
widows in black, pale-faced priests,
tourists in shorts awed by the splendour
and a man who smells of the street.

Santa Maria Maggiore,
a basilica set to music.
Giovanni Pierluigi Palestrina,
wine merchant maestro,
creator of the perfect line,
weaved mysteries here in polyphony.
Perfect lines perfectly joined,
rising with incense in air-borne prayer.
Mathematical beauty intoned –
the voice of the Church forever.

Santa Maria Maggiore,
vault-caressed voices resound it,
warm-veined with quick vibrato:
The Mass of Pope Marcellus –
sublimity tastes worldly like wine.
Gloria in excelsis Deo.
Beautiful words for foreigners,
believers, romantics, lost souls and dreamers.
No meaning, beyond meaning, so very tempting
– o *molto misterioso.*

Basque

Aatxe, shapeshifter, part man, part beast,
avenger of evil and lord of horns,
return to your cave as a young red bull –
to your bachelor bed and goblets of wine.

Mari, scarlet woman – not Maria, blue virgin –
red mare, black he-goat, star of the sea.
Woman-man goddess, ousted queen of your lands,
descend from the mountains bare-breasted in thunder.

Embolden your followers once loved of the gods,
before nature and gender were veiled in lace.
Ave Mari, pray Eve's fallen daughters.
Nature's martyrs are fig-leafed and draped.

Celibate fathers sent desire into hiding,
crimson-torsoletted behind closed doors.
Red-faced bullocks led there by the nose.
Come on big boy, I'm yours, I won't tell.

Mari, rainbow-bedecked, reveal your he-goat;
Aatxe, hoof earth and lower your horns.

Miss Prism's Handbag

Between two glasses of wine,
a sober interregnum.
Red Burgundy sipped in London,
the Rioja in Sussex waiting.

Poets huddle in a Camden church hall,
brave comrades daring to fly.
Outside looks through the window and sees
middle class liberals at prayer.

We disperse to our burrows,
past Londoners in turbans, hijabs and saris;
fun-crowded pubs flying rainbow flags;
on a jukebox, Ziggy still plays guitar;
city lights sparkle with drizzle;
jerk chicken aroma – Jamaica here.
Young faces, excited, out on the town,
their running shoes springboard
into Friday night.

Corkscrews flex in Lewes.
Logs on the fire,
a circle of sofas.
My familiar small town's familiars
wait for me there,
cloistered in terraces on silent streets.

On the train, by the window,
blackened night glass a cinema screen,
editing fellow passengers –
a montage of grainy close ups.

A grey-faced man, grey business-suited,
takes off his tie. Unbuttons his week.
Afternoon-shadow now gangster stubble,
his lager can pull-tab, a champagne cork.
The weekend begins with a serpentine grin.

Two women slip on slurred words,
Excuse me, the fresh-lipsticked mouth,
is there a cocktail bar at Clapham?

I hug the soft Florentine leather.
Inside, a file, my poems collected,
inner-voiced scribbles struggling for meaning
like Oscar Wilde's spinster,
poor driven Miss Prism.
Her life's work – a three-volume novel,
lost from a handbag –
yes, that 'handbag' –
deposited in a cloakroom:
'London Victoria, the Brighton line.'

The bag tries to hide in my lap,
its contents, those poems, have lost their allure.

Let me leave this train at Clapham Junction,
where Oscar Wilde, ruined, stood in his chains.
Let me dump my baggage,
a litter bin will do,
then lose myself
in a cocktail bar.
A cocktail bar?
Yes, Lady Bracknell,
with my new Friday friends.
But not tonight, I'm homeward bound.
I wish them goodbye and they snigger:
What you got in that bag?
The crown jewels?

Nude Ascending a Staircase

Bath towel round the waist
not his style.
He's a body proud guy,
locker-room easy,
a swaggerer – always naked,
even in clothes.
Today he's a fallen Adam
tasting bitter fruit,
feeling sneers
he can't see,
at the foot of the stairs
when the front door slams.

Three floors to climb,
passing fine-art madames,
house-trained nudes
in gilded frames.
Sisters in lines,
forever virginal,
watching.
You there? We should talk?
The towel falls,
he covers his groin.
The answering-machine
a minstrel lament.

A dog lies slumped
on the first-floor landing –
a lookout post,
ten dogs a century.
For two hundred years
a pack of eyes, forensic noses,
superimposed,
watching.
The living dog shivers.

It's alright, boy,
a catch in his voice.
The hunter hunted.

Powdered white, smirking,
dressed in black,
the widow, crinolined,
in daguerreotype.
By her side, fig-leafed,
a bronze warrior torso.
Sophia from Zakynthos,
who lived in this house,
now a hundred years' dead.
She's watching him shrink –
his testes, dead weights,
retreat to their womb.

At the top of the house
the scene of the crime,
a sheet-tangled bed.
Deodorant spray,
a splash of cologne
not covering enough,
he sees who he is.
Here Emmanuelle reigns –
a hallowed film poster –
she frowns,
brazen-breasted,
from her bamboo throne.

Mind the Gap

Rummaging, nosing out, water-dog searching for cerebral
   malfunctions
concealed from brain scans, post-mortem dissections,
bluebottle flies laying maggot eggs, even from deities,
   all-seeing realists.

If this is brain-focused, why do we feel it here in the gut?
   you ask.
Spaniel-like, hypnotised, we have an instinct for decay, we
   predict it.
Something foul in our state, not Denmark alone, but
   everywhere, here within.

Poetry helps, even smiling works, forcing the door when it's
   jammed, slammed shut.
Look out for handrails, they're there for us, frail creatures
   frightened of each other.
Thigh to thigh, buttocks too, trapped here together warm to
   the touch (don't touch).

Listen: 'mind the gap', don't let them push you.
   He died, you know, that man with the voice.
We can't help looking, a habit from childhood days. Upstairs
   bus-views, nose-squeezed.
Buckingham Palace walled, princesses looked out for
   excitement.

Forget the fetid smell, it isn't real. Really? You sure of
   that? Imagine.
Midnight skin glistening, we swim paths moonlight cast.
You're
   smiling, spaniel-eyed.

Crouching Tigers

The first salute to the sun;
a doctor closes the screen.

Naked and broken under white cotton,
a fallen combatant mourns his defeat;
the iron hammer sinks in the river.

Remembered muscles reconnect with the sky;
hands like sunflowers twist on their stalks.

'Can you feel this?' No gloves this time;
the hungry tiger grasps the goat.
Feet exposed, held, fingernail traced.

The golden cockerel stands on one leg;
The left knee bends to carry the weight,
the right raised high *en garde*.

A kick, when it comes, is parried –
the warriors matched.
The first punch fails – and the second.

They crouch coiled, bamboo dappled,
alert to each breath. Unblinking eyes
a silent fanfare. The next move the last.

Twin dragons rush out to sea.

Medical fingers examine the spine,
a rock-climber feeling for cracks,
flinching when I flinch, reading braille.
The exhalation – his or mine?

A thoracic vertebrae fracture, he says,
hands stretched upwards to dry in the air.
The final salute to the sun.

The white cranes soar to the sky;
a breeze rustles the bamboo leaves.

Aleppo
After Lawand al-Attar

Scream mouth if you can,
stretch back lips,
diaphragm and lungs cry horror.

Eyelids shut by masonry dust,
ears search inwards
sealed by an unheard dirge.

Fragments of home coat your face like a mask.
Cry without tears, shout without words.

Vision narrows to close-down,
fear penetrates beyond nostril-deep.

Stumble forward, escape the darkness.
Your face a void, arms hang loose,
legs try to crumple but daren't.

Voices call you out from the ruins,
no longer home – darkness bleeds tears.
Tread ankle deep where black dilutes red.

Spot-lit from the front, there can be no cover.
Naked through rags, bones bleach, cameras flash.
Look down and help us look away.
We too are stumbling, escaping the light.
More frightening than black is white.

Waiting

No public access where they took him.
Three-thirty or three-forty?
It doesn't matter, he said.
Three-thirty it was, in February drizzle,
waiting on plastic upholstery by a bronchial automatic door
opening and closing for old folk on sticks,
framing daffodil buds and puddles.
The sun's trying to come out.
Caution slippery floor.
Is this still your address?
The others in rows by the daytime TV.
It's better away from the draught.
Cover your cough.
Sandwich bar closed.
How's Sam these days?
He's a bit smelly, that's all.
Wasn't he your mum's dog, before...?
English Fern cologne from the chemist's tester.
A bit strong we'd thought this morning.
Fortunate now, lingering here,
masking hospital fragrance of pine.
He's gorgeous, my grandson, in America.
That's nice.
I filled up a wine bottle, you know.
I bet that was uncomfortable.
Filled it right up. Couldn't get to the bathroom.
She doesn't come here anymore.
He's behind the blue door.
No public access.
The nurse smiles and looks at her watch...
Cheery blue woodwork and turquoise walls;
cheery, they thought.
Not today.

Sicilian Vespas

The shadow, a shiver by the Tyrrhenian Sea
on a raisin-plump island sweet with Marsala –
a Mafia-scarred land, stoic in grief.
There's no shade here but my Panama hat;
today, like a Sicilian, I'm living with ghosts.
Ancient gods, please, smile on this land,
on all Sicilians, tragedy's heirs,
Normans, Arabs, Phoenicians and Greeks.
Bestow on them your gifts of peace.
Give them laughter, cannoli and Vespa scooters.

I stand on one leg, foot buried in sand –
Taichi in Cefalù out-staring the sea.
An old woman there with prophetic eyes.
Her nest a blanket, children orbiting wild.
She wears black, her smile a crack
on a face engraved with sun and sorrow.
A hesitant warrior preparing to jump,
I tilt and wobble, leaping forward a step.
She laughs without teeth, gums watermelon red.
For a moment, she frightens the children, who stare.

Mount Etna's precipice, perilous, dares me.
Here I sense endings as summer dissolves.
Colour-blinded, eyes sharp-focus, monochromed.
Below, villages vanish in mist.
Boots crunch invisible through gaseous steam,
the march through clouds is solemn and silent.
Heads down, silhouetted, in single-file,
we tourists are treading the top of the World.
The Sun feigns its death as a warning.
There at the Earth heart, the long haemorrhage.

Sand-warmed but volcano-sobered
on the beach by the fortress' ancient ruin,
I listen as church bells toll evening vespers.
The woman packs up bambini and bags.
I sink to a crouch, low monkey stance,
back straight, palms sarcophagal,
a wall-gazing monk, feet island-rooted.
Young men on scooters, in suntans and shorts,
fire up lazy engines trailing lazier laughter.
The sun drops seawards like a blood-orange ball.

Butterfly
for Bill Hemmig

Apollo in disguise, Lieutenant Pinkerton,
New World hero, his glamour glittering.
An American eagle drawn to the light,
his wings, outstretched fans, shadow the globe.

Earthbound, circling, diving, recircling,
their more-than-desire fuels his descent.
Always this, his ritual bride's vision.

Paradise birds silenced, eclipse at high noon;
jasmine and verbena perfume his path;
Pinkerton here – he returns with the spring.

Blossom-veiled, shining rapturous pink,
Madam Butterfly awaits her sanctified spouse.
They meet – home again – in the orchard –
reunited, reconsecrated, consumed by fire.

Cio-Cio San under the cherry tree,
Madam Butterfly, solemn in silk,
mahogany eyes scan a grey seascape.
Her winter vigil is lit from within.

This bud burst – call it a mood,
this consummation – call it a dream.

Her deepest wound is congealing,
the future no longer a void.
What was and what will be merge –
knowledge is the present tense.

Not a flash of beauty on the cusp of a season,
not a thrill on the passing breeze,
she sees it again, and again –
cherry-blossom fired.

Love makes you strong, Cio-Cio San.

Under the tree Pinkerton is part of you,
your roots intertwine. He can never leave.

You're not so fragile, Cio-Cio San.

Shed tears, if you will, as the blossom falls,
papering you pink in a petal cascade.

The Samurai knife returns to its sheath.

Now you can see what the tree saw:
Pinkerton here, like you, cherry-stained.

Be still in this moment. Lie at peace in his lap.

Mollusc

Spent juices mark its progress
in a trail of glistening slime.
Slowly it advances, antennae alert,
mysteriously tracking with radar,
salivating to nestle in green.

Single-minded desire drives the beast,
arrow-straight and appetite-aimed,
over a thousand molluscan miles.
Intoxicated, shell-reinforced, blind
to the threat of the dart-eyed bird.

A word-wounded man, camouflage-fatigued,
stumbles nowhere, hiding tears
not allowed – not for him.
His unhappiness crustacean grim,
anger boils in Doc Martin boots.

He kicks.

The stone, Palaeolithic,
axe-headed, ricochets.
The soft-feathered blackbird,
flexed to dive, flees.
The snail persists.

On this summer-hushed day, hope is crushed.

The Battle of Princeton

Princeton Gothic the ivy-clad college,
mirage-blurred on a siesta day,
summer-vacated, horse-fly invaded,
stately lawns of gentrified grass,
dappled by branches of long-memoried trees.

A placid town proud of its battle scar,
the single cannonball that routed the British,
fox-chased here by Washington's men.
Two hundred redcoats, a long way from home,
admitting defeat with a limp white rag.

Briefcase pillowed under a buttonwood tree,
a middle-aged male, grey-suited, lies splayed
with dress shirt slippage, hints of flesh.
A drowsy arm's stretch from browsable bookshops,
an Englishman has fallen in battle again.

Hummingbird Feeder

A sanctuary, the New Jersey porch,
wisteria branches cling colonnaded,
a wicker table set hospitably,
temperature sultry,
gin icy,
the dash of bitters, a sanguinary note.

I flew there once in July.

Sheltering there too
the hummingbird feeder,
sucrose nectar in
brightly red plastic,
drunk on the wing
by frantic creatures
sustained by sweetness.

The Blueberry Cage
For Ila Pearl

You don't need a road to get home.
My guide, the child, an adventure-trekker.
I shed the years with my shoes,
we wade ankle-deep down the creek.
Solemn-faced, she tells me the rules:
Look out for snakes but don't be afraid.

I follow her track from the blueberry cage,
pannier baskets piled high with purple,
feast day promises, escorted by bees,
through brittle grasses, buzzing.
Then relief from the heat, straw hat fanned,
iced lemon tea under perfumed viburnum.

A small mucky hand brings another surprise.
My tutor, self-appointed, skips from the barn.
Look through these, you can see the bug.
An insect dead behind a cracked lens,
Ila Pearl's world through plastic binoculars.
Wonder in a desiccated beetle.

Desert Nights
for Linda Bell

Flashing yellow and black, strobing the moon,
the neon night, California-grilled,
sweats its fever through my motel window
with Budweiser laughter, trumpet-mellowed.

A man howls wolf, his jeans distressed denim,
chest-hugged by his contoured guitar,
strumming tremoloed strings in 4/4 time,
crooning the blues, raspy, on a spot-lit bed.

On another night, another moon
polished our bodies, you and I,
chiaroscuro'd on sand dunes
under stars defined as propitious.

Straightening the sheet on the unmade bed,
I relight that moon with a single finger.
An unbroken line on wind-smoothed sand,
my tremulous calligraphy, a promise.

Dido in Carthage

Is there a photograph?
You where I stood
looking for new worlds

before we met.
I prayed blindly humble,
air-borne knowledge came in peace.

We bathed in nothing there.
Opened arms hushed those first messages
Now no native land can claim us.

Why tears? Crying clouds alone in the hall.
Mirrors like us strong.
They unlock that place so far away.

First a ghostly form of you –
lost hands, your face, blossom flushed muscles.
Who gave me this alchemy, these dreams?

I shiver, calm, singed by cold flames.
The future has time enough.
Enough fuel for forlorn beginnings.

In this city forever yours,
long hairless memories hide naked,
sweat, half-remembered, smells of human malaise.

Mirrored images in perfumed gardens.
Where the fountain died, statues crumble.
Build the fire here and stack it high.

The Awakening

Sleeping, muttering, he smiles,
lightly covered by the Indian cotton
they'd bought together at a bazaar.
Warm in early morning sunlight,
muscles loosen forgotten limbs
drawn in dreams towards familiar flesh.
Eyelids register red then gold,
sunbeams gild hairs on an outstretched arm.

Cotton-tangled feet kick off the sheet;
skin, exposed, no longer hugged,
dries on the breath of the breeze
whispered through last night's opened window.
Sleep's smile melts to a gathering frown,
gold turns blue and eyelids unshutter.
No dawn chorus – a blackbird shriek –
a man, alone, awakes.

Looking for Fernando Pessoa

Mother dear, beloved,
how many times can you leave me?
What must I do to be yours?
Show me my father as he was to you –
the beautiful man who left us behind.
No, not the lover, his body is yours.

If my legacy's not in your gift,
let me be the raggedy tramp.

How to hide pin-pricked eyes
and ventriloquist-sullen lips?
How many masquerade faces
to conceal these orphanage wounds?
There are many amputations repeated
on the journey to approximate manhood.

How to create the man
when the child is already lost?

Here in the joke-shop, Groucho Marx's disguise:
the glasses, clip-on nose and comic moustache.

Don't tell me you love me.
Don't explain why you don't.
I won't look behind your harem of veils.
Let me be Charlie and Groucho,
not a celluloid Valentino –
I am that man on the tram.

So many ways to hide the truth
– not enough words to find it.

The Odalisque

Lying here naked on the old chaise longue,
I unsmile the smile he says he can't see,
unfocusing my eyes inflames his fetish.

Here on his libido's red velvet throne,
safely elevated from aesthetic small talk,
I try to guess what he really wants.

Why so Chaplinesque, my shy Buster Keaton?
Silent movies say more than you think.
Should I close my thighs as well as my mouth?

Resisting the itch on restive buttocks,
I lie here blanked by his cryptic lenses,
refusing to mirror those primly pursed lips.

I pretend I'm flattered to be crowned his muse –
but I'd rather unzip his dark-suited ego and
ask him which way, if he dared, he would do it.

Rosarium

1. Falstaff

Swollen proud on the stem, his plumes pumped,
a Plantagenet cavalier doused in eau de toilette
clambers Sussex flint walls, stretching for light.
Old rose heraldry Agincourt-thorned.

No honourable knight comes armed with secateurs,
battle-blades set on amputation. These blooms,
louchely hanging, seduce buzzing warriors –
not intended to wilt severed in a single stem vase.

Nature's punishment is well-deserved.
Surgical slashes gash flesh to the quick.
Justice pronounced on bandage stains,
crimson, passion's colour, congeals darkly purple.

This hunter's trophy better than tiger skin
or the wall-mounted head of an open-mouthed stag.

2. Golden Celebration

Here goes, my brave boys!
a ring of bells spreads the news.
Gilded buds clammer: *We're here!*
The first-born siblings' tenor toll.

A surprise, this rose-decked shrub,
golden-ribboned for Father's Day.
A filial gesture, Magus treasure,
planted in fertile soil.

Buds pipe: *I as treble do begin.*
Blooms intone: *Unto church I call.*
Petals shrivel on swollen stems:
Ring a ring o' roses. We all fall down.

Nature's rota. A carillon call.
Listen. Nose-smothered. Inhale.

3. Danse de Feu

Midnight, illuminated by lightning,
bedroom-trapped, I watch him,
bleached scarlet, strobed,
clinging cruciform on ancient flint.

Poi fire balls, whiplashed, spin
aboriginal patterns, war paint,
processional drums thrill away sleep.
Dare to join the fiesta.

Red is for stop and for danger –
we recoil from the colour of blood.
On our knees, we learnt to be scared.
I will join him out there in the storm.

Daybreak perfumed with loam,
the fire dance, sunlit, burns.

4. Iceberg

We wake cold in our beds. Nightmares of icebergs.
Splintering steel, death by drowning,
giant molars grind ships lost in the storm.
The Polar North fractures. Unnatural warming.

Glacial mountains float in Newfoundland waters,
a washing-line view when pegging out sheets.
Billowing cotton stirs pioneer memories,
a widow watches the albatross swoop.

Doomed polar bears hitch lifts to oblivion,
the great journey south, a liquid rebirth.
Defrosted water, hurricane-stirred,
blown eastwards, hurtling on thunder clouds.

Iceberg juice sprinkled on Whitsun-frocked flowers –
Asperges showers. Sussex summer, Arctic-born.

5. Benjamin Britten

Bass drum. Thunder crack. Then a gong prolonged.
Silence in a cymbal trill. Hush, the violins high.
Pink. Orange. Om. Zen. Yes, go on, flash us your red.
Sweet fearsome Ben, his eyes were ears, his ears eyes.

Peter. Lost. Peter? Who? Lonely Peter Grimes drowned.
Or Peter loved? Peter Pears, Ben's voice on Earth.
Pink. Orange. Om. Zen. Yes, go on, flash us your red.
Spring cuckoo gone. Ding dong. Ben's summer trumpet.

No rose of swych virtu – harmony for discordant times.
What colour Ben? Red under the bed, white feather scorned.
Pink. Orange. Om. Zen. Yes, go on, flash us your red.
Ben, rainbow brother, illegal lover, radical gamelan guy.

Let's hear it for Ben and his chameleon-coloured music.
Yes, go on. Brass fanfare. Glockenspiel. Timpani roll.

Gardening Tip

Virgin shoots flex promises.
No matter. Seasons break their word.
Horticulture signs no affidavits,
fresh-sprung leaves tease,
forsythia yellow is an acid sneer.

We plant daffodil bulbs in autumn
trying to ease our malaise.
When dog daisies blacken with frost
we rekindle gold rush dreams,
our fingers warmed in frozen earth.

Lewes Castle

William de Warrene, the Conqueror's mate,
one of those Norman aristo arrivistes,
looks down at us from his hilltop ruin.
We conquered classes sometimes look back.

Lewes Castle knows how to pose.
High on the mound, it sucks in its stomach,
flexed pectorals, buttocks clenched,
crooning oldie-world ballads at teatime.

We see what we want in its hollow shell –
lords and ladies, Hollywood style,
pantomime villains on plywood thrones,
headless knights, haunted suits of armour.

No longer a threat to rebels or serfs,
William's stronghold is open for business –
civil unions, even commoners' weddings,
amateur theatricals and arty craft fairs.

Foreign students squint, smartphone snapping,
Hard Rock t-shirts on pigeon chests,
sneakered feet scuffing cobbled stones,
romancing the ruins with ice-cream moustaches.

Restive children in hi-vis jackets,
led to the precipice by teacher adventurers,
learn history's message in a tangle of limbs,
their screams fail to frighten the ravens.

Later in moonlight, William de Warrene returns,
the 1066 victor, not quite forgotten,
battlement spooky for strollers
on a slow-march home from the pub.

In Kiln Wood

Here woodland men tamed chestnut and hornbeam.
These woods are haunted by blackened faces
memorialised in old coppiced trees,
cut for new growth, they never grow old –
reborn over centuries for burning in kilns.

Wellington boots snap summer-dried sticks
left in the mud by short-memoried dogs.
Humans still an intrusion here,
startling unseen woodlanders, missiled voles,
rummaging blackbirds as noisy as boars.

An old fox, grizzled, fire-eyed, suspicious,
sniffs the air and merges with bracken.
Postcard-pert, a robin is singing
cascading notes, certainly not love songs.
He is laying claim to my green rubber boots,
ploughing my furrow, churning up grubs.

Walking here with my lifetime of dogs,
I make tentative imprints in untrodden snow,
watching my step through ghost-faced anemones,
and punctual to their seasons, bluebells in mists,
red fruits with evil propositions, sly belladonna,
mushroom zombies rising up through the mulch.

The robin retreats to his tree, worm-trophied,
no retrospection for a small hunter-gatherer
soon chased away by a rival male,
blood on the redbreast – a new burst of song.

Galloping, panting, spaniel-ears flapping,
my current dog returns like the many before him.
Imagined prey retrieved in triumph,
a coppiced stick newly-dead in his maw.

November Landscape
for Dawn Stacey

The raptor-eyed painter in wax waterproofs –
moisture sheened, she's striding with dogs.
A Derbyshire woman on Sussex chalk hills
foraging for images with steam engine breath.

A hilltop castle dyed red from the East,
spider-slung nets shine polished steel.
No flowers, just seed heads,
no leaves where the birds are.

Skeleton trees scratch streaks in the sky,
the nest deserted, a crown of thorns,
that marbled jade egg, a solitary grave.
Shadow of crow, pink cumulus-framed.

Fallen chestnuts lie afield with berries.
Where the cold roses are, blackbirds scrummage.
Bramblings flit from bulrush to teasel,
thrushes' beaks rake up leaves, finding snails.

The canvas a chorus of separate parts:
a feather, a leaf, a rosehip cluster.
Hedgerows and coppices painted in boxes,
November defined with a forensic brush.

Waterlogged

Damp under buttock but solid enough,
an old wooden seat, half-hearted refuge.
The bank erodes where the old chair's enthroned –
impatient these currents of diluted mud.
Tidal rivers shrug off picturesque.
There are lovelier places but they are elsewhere.

Tearful willows bathe listless branches;
poplars, in pairs, cast silhouette daubs
on a Delft china sky patched up with clouds.
Rosebay Willow herbs, mauve-coiffured punks,
loiter with hawthorns, now bundles of sticks
and sharp-toothed nettles that lurk thigh-high.

Tangled weeds sweep past me like thoughts.
Anonymous ghosts washed down to Shallot,
a Raglan cardigan weighed down with stones,
baby Moses capsized in the rushes,
no mermaids here, they're full fathom five.
Waterlogged, drowning, my hands clench the bench.

Baritone banter provokes a scene change.
Loose-limbed rafters, barefoot-balanced,
harmonise their laughter, walking on water,
gondoliering, speeding, with testosterone gusto.
Doused with their backsplash, I re-join the path,
barge-horse contented, my boots gravel-crunch.

Postcards

We meet best like this – on doormats.
You exploding among brown envelopes
shouting out summer on dismal days.
You send me skies painted blue,
Italian seascapes, cathedral spires,
sunflower heads jostling for light.
I warm my hands on your holiday postcards
wishing we could talk as photograph clear.

Sète

Slate grey winter dissolves.
Water-coloured smudges
animate rain-coated streets,
would-be rivers' puddled mirages.
The pedestrian hiatus camouflaged
by denim and old stressed leather,
working gear with a dash of chic.
Blue meets black, shrugged
on slated chairs outside café-bars.
Pastis apéritifs diluted with water
glow deceitfully yellow,
tasted between cigarette breaths.
Today's news digested in the *Midi Libre*,
reddening blood in monochrome.

Led to what might have been
down tree-dormant avenues
observed from above
by branch-perched crows –
ennui-stunned, even taxidermal.
Pursued by whispers, espresso coloured,
alerted to the unseen by the unknown,
finding traces of nothing
in the silence of water
on a rented balcony with a harbour view.
Fishing boats, returned on the morning tide,
fragment into abstractions, gold to brown.
Marina-cradled, herring gull cruised,
beauty makes hostages of those who stare.

Mortwick Village

Don't talk to strangers in polo neck sweaters.
I was a child when my aunt told me this.
The man on the beach seemed friendly enough.
Maybe his smile was more of a grin.
We can learn from the greetings of strangers.

Good morning, they say here in the mornings;
then *Good afternoon,* after lunch.
Everyone smiles in the street.
Another fine day. Aren't we lucky.
No polo neck sweaters in this village.

Public civility, is it sincere?
You won't ever leave, sounds ominous here.
Unsolicited beverages over the fence.
Don't take coffee from strangers
– with or without polo necks.

Strychnine with caffeine, a cruel deceit.
Living in villas, in a village of villas.
More coffee, sherry, beers round the fire.
Questions, always questions,
and the covert meetings of eyes.

Never trust strangers in groups
when you are the guest at the hearth.
In this village of villas, a new face appears.
He smiles, shy in his polo neck sweater.
The neighbours invite him to tea.

The Storm Brewed

A cup without a saucer is a lonely sight
– sadder than a saucer without a cup.
Limoges, reproduction, the tea-trolley grail,
not dishwasher-proof – handle with care.
Immortal the person who breaks it.

A union shattered, a tea party ruined.
The saucer a jigsaw of purple and gold,
the cup now a relic, a widowed consort,
pushed to the back of the cupboard,
the imperial augur, an omen of ruin.

A black cat, unseen, battlefield veteran,
anarchist beast, suspected street saboteur,
harbinger of good fortune as well as of evil,
unimpressed by drawing-room dramas and farces,
laps up spilt milk with a venomless tongue.

Ansel

The elevator panel lights up at L,
a robotic voice sneers *Lower Ground Floor*.
Big Ben strikes a curt 3 o'clock.
Late lunch with Eleanor.
Her white box apartment –
right-angled, uncluttered – Le Corbusier style.
Eleanor's hospitality is minimalist too:
lettuce, herrings and chilled Muscatel.
Heloise, lacrosse heroine from lost lycée days,
crashes onto the scene like a learner-driver
bringing scarlet orchids with sepals erect
and air-kissing lips, cellophane sealed.

Ansel's smile, silver-framed behind glass,
is released from the drawer by Eleanor's bed.
His face lurks too in the golden heart locket
that glitters on Heloise's décolletage.
She fondles it lightly letting Eleanor talk.
Melancholy eyes mourn sisterhood lost,
impossible to hide the unpalatable truth.
There's an elephant in Eleanor's L-shaped room.

Sortie

It doesn't exist, no harm, so inhale it.
Gitanes, unfiltered, your last cigarette.
A Fedora, brim down, plucked from the rain
with a shabby trench coat – Bogart chic.
T-shirt, trainers and frayed blue denim,
everything hidden, you descend underground.
La vie en monochrome. Was it Truffaut's
fault? Indulging this fetish in ennui.
Sartre's no help, his hand on your spine,
pushing. No Train. They don't stop here.
This Parisian moment on an empty stage,
a last inhalation with dry ice smoke,
entente d'accordéon, Brel *ne me quitte pas.*
Climb back to your personal circle of hell.

Eve

He'd left Eden neglected
when he fell,
tree-nest bereft,
feet concrete-set.

Gone.

Eve saw the end,
ever the sleek,
serpent-tempted femme.
Left there
with all the work –

She's next.

Proffer Your Hand

Let me take your pulse,
I want to feel your voice.
Allow me to touch
where rivers converge
under drum-skin.
Here a messenger pleads
unspoken thoughts,
ambiguities in eyes.
A fingertip on flesh
detects Morse Code.
Let me take your pulse.
Proffer your hand,
palm open, exposed.

Entanglement

A subtle trap, this two-way affair,
predator and victim declassified.
Synchronised muscles flex and respond
to whispered breath, flesh premonitions.

Messages transmit down wireless threads,
each fingertip touch puppeteer-mastered.
The smallest gestures unleash giants,
convulsions born on a butterfly's wing.

So easily spun, with no unravelling,
invisible strands ensnared us here.
Each move, each glance, each premeditation,
pulls at the knot, entangling us tighter.

A fearful embracing, relentless death throes,
concealed, cocooned and suspended in silk.

Time Travels

We walk, lingering,
you and me,
where cherry trees fruit.
I join me there,
looking for a fight.
My solitary shadow
a jagged blade
fallen unused at my feet.

I find that orchard again,
alone with a drone of wasps.
They return too, you and I.
We three
weaponless now,
walking on cherries.
Prophecy remembered –
we look away.

My Seat in the Quire

No virgins they –
spread-legged on a tombstone
by the ragged yew tree.
'Magic' they say,
talking of lager
on the mortal remains of a brewer.
Teenage soundtracks
in the churchyard.
An mp3 download –
Madonna remixed.

A minute's silence
inside the church,
St Mary the Virgin, C of E.
The boys have gone
(they think I'm the vicar).
Enclosed in Perpendicular Gothic,
I'm tempted to kneel
on a pew consecrated with *Pledge*.

Words whispered in youth
in a place like this
(vows, I thought then)
come back to me now,
uninvited and unintended.
They float somewhere,
up there,
in high-vaulted space.

Sancta Maria have mercy on me
and all those who lie buried here –
quacks, alchemists and vicars,
Virginia tobacco manufacturers,
African explorers, that brewer too
– once honoured dream-makers all.

Is it a trick of the light?

Kneeling here now,
smelling lavender polish,
I greet *art nouveau* saints,
evening-lit, and, on a
long breath, intone *Nunc dimittis.*
Now lettest thou thy servant depart in peace.

At the Crossroads

A mild-mannered explorer
journeyed without compass,

stumbling, mocked and bloodied,
on the road from there to here.

The transmogrification his agony.

Friends couldn't stop him;
they could only mourn.

He arrived blinded by sunlight.

Verification at the crossroads,
metamorphosis in a cloud of dust,

epiphany in a meeting –
fellow travellers on Damascene quests.

The stranger shrugged nonchalantly,
benediction in his laugh.

Bonjour Monsieur. Bienvenue.

October 30th 2008
for the NHS staff at Royal Sussex County Hospital, Brighton

Unlit logs stacked in the grate
predict this evening's pleasures,
wine-warmed, watching well-meaning flames;
night cordite-scented with noisy stardust.
Vegetative lanterns grin and grimace,
the walking dead up late, tricking or treating
before the saints come marching in
– *Oompah, oompah, boom boom boom* –
comfort in cheery pumpkin time.

Baritone karaoke sweeping the house:
here's Verdi's Rigoletto
La-ra, la-ra, la-ra.
Passionate jester with dustpan and brush
La-ra, la-ra, la-ra.
After the dust storm, emails transmitted,
wise-crack jokes sent into space.
None of them matter. That's the jest.
La-ra, la-ra, la-ra.

October's last days curl up purring,
tranquil endings gathered in.
This morning is for treats –
please, no more tricks.
Coffee-time is imminent.

Pain comes from nowhere.
Instant night somewhere on stairs.
A movie clip on the cutting-room floor.

The call for help, another sequence,
on a phone, on the bed, without a lamp.
Disconnected beads strung on razor wire,
necklaced in chains, struggling for sense.

The doctor in a doorway, lit from behind;
an ambulance ceiling, paramedical faces;
images stretchered away on a trolley.
More faces, some familiar –
an African man, worried, smiles:
Can you feel this?
Voice calm, kind without hope,
fading to black.
Not much more than nothing.

It is only a game – *Super Mario Galaxy* –
he remembers the tune, not his avatar's name.
The mouse woman (is she a rat?)
a bad guy with a monstrous head.
She walks up and down, patrolling, uniformed;
a soldier, busy, she can't see him now.
He knows it's not good because of the hum –
constant, ominous, the smell of bad news.

Are you alright? Mouse woman asks with a smile.
Where is this? Who am I meant to be?
She holds his hand.
Not a game then.
The hum's not a hum, it is pain.

He looks at himself spread out on a bed,
tubes where no tubes have been before.
His clothes gone. Where? How?
The gown doesn't meet at the back.

Not a game then.
Not a game, a hospital ward,
night-light obscured, shadows not shapes.
Men sleep in beds, gurgling dreams.
Half-seeing, he knows where he is:
moonlit on a battlefield
with the dead and the dying.

Awaiting fate in a place unknown.
Nowhere to hide from the hum.

He will never remember those six lost hours –
epileptic ferocity, flailing limbs,
the choreography snapping his spine.
Now he knows how the movie will end:
flooded with blood in a crimson burst,
the brain simply flicks the switch.
Drama turned off, time to go.

Consciousness was once a creature of air,
incorporeal, floating free
far above anatomy.
So he'd thought.

Now it looks at the world through an open wound.
A half-inflated football, his thinking-machine,
the shrivelled walnut of medical books,
kicked to Earth, reborn in star bursts.
He is who he is – a man of flesh –
not Super Mario.
He may never get to Level Three
and if, in the end, there's no celestial choir,
no golden glow when the lights go out,
he won't be there to regret it.

Toes grip the ground, lungs fill with air,
he greets the unseen sky.
Inside, at his centre, a new sensation.
The crescendo starts pianissimo,
exciting even in the moment of birth.
A morphine cocktail from a plastic glass.
His body's chorus is singing again.

One year later in shortened days,
pumpkins and fireworks. No marching saints.
Another trick. Maybe a treat.

The end postponed, the song returns –
Rigoletto trills over his coffee
La-ra, la-ra, la-ra.
Humming alone in a small café.
Another October morning.

In Extremis

The waking a shock, another place interrupted,
above my head, a part of me,
more than brain, not just mind, a halo.

I lie here, a stretchered case,
intensively cared-for, fluids syringed,
vampire-needles, strangers stethoscope-hung.
Patient 2514579, a statistic tucked up in bed.

I'm here with the dying,
entangled with tubes.
Skittles fall, they're wheeled away.
The conveyor belt is uninterrupted -
clean sheets, pillows buffed,
the *nil by mouth* sign removed.

No time for talking, I've morphine for company.
Cheers, everyone! No one hears.
Angels are human, B-list actors in cameo roles.
Medication makes me star of my show,
days and nights strobe my eyes.

No-time later, a nurse draws the curtains,
I think of nets in living-room windows.
A man appears, white-coat crisp, brown hands warm,
his voice too. I've seen him before,
when my stretcher came in from the cold.

That should feel better.
Simple words, no heavenly choirs,
tears come and I see gold.

Notes

p.8 'Four-Minute Song'
'Epilogue' from *Day by Day* by Robert Lowell (Farrar Straus Giroux, 1977).
'Those blessed structures, plot and rhyme –
Why are they no help to me now.'

p.16 'Naked Man'
The American poets Allen Ginsberg and Peter Orlovsky were longtime partners.

p.24 'Society Contracts'
Enoch Powell (1912-1998) was a British Conservative politician. 'All political lives...end in failure, because that is the nature of politics and of human affairs.' *Joseph Chamberlain* by Enoch Powell (Thames and Hudson, 1977).

p.26 'A Step Away from Frank'
'A Step Away from Them' is a poem in *Lunch Poems* by Frank O'Hara (City Lights Books, 1964).
Jim McGuinn, known as Roger McGuinn, was the lead singer and guitarist from The Byrds (1964-1973).
Joni Mitchell's song 'Woodstock' (1969):
'We are stardust/We are golden/And we've got to get ourselves/Back to the garden.'

p.30 'Outside the Cathedral'
Prega per noi peccatori (Pray for us sinners) from the Italian translation of the Ave Maria.
The Italian composer Giovanni Pierluigi da Palestrina (c.1525-1594) was director of music at the 5th century basilica of Santa Maria Maggiore, in Rome. His mass, *Missa Papae Marcelli* (Pope Marcellus Mass), is highly regarded as a supreme example of polyphonic church music. Palestrina married the rich widow of a wine merchant in 1581.

p.32 'Basque'
Aatxe and Mari are characters from Basque mythology.
Aatxe is a shapeshifting spirit. He can be a man or a young red bull. Mari is the principal goddess in Basque mythology. She is often represented as a red cow or a black he-goat.

p.33 'Miss Prism's Handbag'
Oscar Wilde stayed in the seaside town of Worthing, Sussex, when writing his play, *The Importance of Being Earnest*. Trains from Victoria go to Worthing, Brighton and Lewes. Also on the Brighton line is Clapham Junction where Oscar Wilde waited for the train that would take him to Reading Gaol in 1895.

p.38 'Crouching Tigers'
The italicised phrases refer to various moves in the Chinese White Crane 'soft' martial art form known as *Shuang Yang*.

p.40 'Aleppo'
After an untitled painting by the Aleppo-born Syrian artist Lawand al-Attar at his 2013 London exhibition, *Equinox* (The Mosaic Rooms, London).

p.42 'Sicilian Vespas'
The Sicilian Vespers is the name given to the successful rebellion against the occupying French on the island of Sicily that broke out on Easter Day, 1282.

p.44 'Butterfly'
Madama Butterfly (1904) is an Italian opera by Giacomo Puccini (1858-1924).

p.47 'The Battle of Princeton'
At the Battle of Princeton (1777), General George Washington defeated the British army near the town of Princeton, New Jersey. Before surrendering, 200 British soldiers took refuge in the town's Nassau Hall, now at the centre of the Princeton University campus.

p.51 'Dido in Carthage'
Dido was the first queen of Carthage and is best remembered for her passionate but ultimately tragic relationship with the hero, Aeneas, in Virgil's *Aeneid*. Jupiter orders Aeneas to leave Dido, and Dido commits suicide on a funeral pyre.

p.53 'Looking for Fernando Pessoa'
Fernando Pessoa (1888-1935) was a Portuguese Modernist poet who frequently wrote under the different names of 75 invented characters.

pp.55-57 'Rosarium'
Rosarium is the Latin word for a rose garden. The titles of these five poems are roses that grow in my own rose garden.
'Golden Celebration': The phrases in italics are names given to various rings, or peals, of bells.
'Benjamin Britten' (1913-1976) was an English composer. Among his many operas are *Peter Grimes*, *Billy Budd*, and *Owen Wingrave*. He wrote many operatic roles for his lifetime partner, the tenor Peter Pears (1910-1986)

p.59 'Lewes Castle'
Lewes Castle, in Lewes, Sussex, was built in 1069 by William de Warrenne (died 1088), 1st Earl of Surrey, the son-in-law of William The Conqueror, three years after the Norman Invasion of England.

p.64 'Sète'
Sète is a port and seaside resort, situated on the Mediterranean, in the Occitanie region of Southern France.

p.68 'Sortie'
The black and white film, *Les Quatre Cents Coups* (*The 400 Blows*, 1959) by Francois Truffaut (1932–1984) is considered the first film of the French New Wave. The French Existentialist philosopher, Jean-Paul Sartre (1905-1980) wrote 'Hell is other people' ('L'Enfer, c'est les autres') in his play *Huis Clos* (*No Exit*) first performed in 1944.
'Ne me quitte pas' ('Don't leave me', 1959) is a song by the Belgian singer-songwriter, Jacques Brel (1929-1978).

p.76 'October 30th 2008'
La-ra, la-ra, la-ra from the scena and aria *Povero Rigoletto… Cortigiani, vil razza dannata* the opera *Rigoletto* (1851) by Giuseppe Verdi.
Super Mario Galaxy was a video game by Nintendo, released in 2007.

Acknowledgements

Several poets and friends have helped and encouraged me during the interesting times (from 2008 onwards) when I was writing these poems: Peter Abbs, Julie Adams, Patrick Bond, Julian Boughton, Lisa Dart, Mary-Jane Grandinetti, Bill Hemmig, Chris Iles, Andie Lewenstein, Paul Matthews, John McCullough, Ruth O'Callaghan, Belinda Singleton and Kay Syrad. My wife, Linda Bell, has been supportive and patient during this time too. Many thanks to you all.

Thanks also to Adele Ward and Mike Wood from Ward Wood Publishing for the many pleasures of being published by them, with special thanks to Adele Ward who has not just been my publisher and friend, but who was the first person to suggest that I should write poetry.

The following poems, in various versions, originally appeared in these publications – I am grateful to the editors for their support:
'The Sea Says' and 'The Tale of An Apple and A Sausage' appeared in *The Blotter Magazine*, November issue, 2009.
'The Great Escape' and 'High-Flyer' were published by Muse-Pie Press in *Shot Glass Journal* – Issue 3 (2011) and Issue 6 (2012).
'Haiku', 'Wrestling Angels', 'Sicilian Vespas', 'The Blueberry Cage' and 'Hummingbird Feeder' were first published by *Every Day Poets* in 2011-2013.
'Mollusc' was included in the anthology *Genius Floored: Uncurtained Window*, by Soaring Penguin Press, 2013.
'Home Movie' was anthologised by Cinnamon Press in *Reaching Out*, 2013.
'Four-Minute Song' first appeared in *Shot Glass Journal* Issue 10 (2013). Also published in *The Needlewriters* by The Frogmore Press, 2015.
'Basque' was published by Soaring Penguin Press in the anthology *Whispers in Smoke*, 2014.
'Gardening Tip' was included in the anthology *The Four Seasons*, Kind of a Hurricane Press, 2015.

About the Author

Colin Bell was born in a Franciscan convent in Surrey but grew up in Sussex – everything that he has done, he did for the first time in Brighton. After half a lifetime in Manchester working for Granada Television, he returned to Sussex and now lives in Lewes, the urban equivalent of BBC Radio Four.

His poetry has been published in the UK and the US by Cinnamon Press, Soaring Penguin Press, Muse-Pie Press, Bittersweet, Kind of A Hurricane Press and The Blotter. He has been nominated in the US for the Pushcart Prize in 2016 and 2019. Many of his Fibonacci poems have been published in *The Fib Review* and have been set to music by American composer Tim Risher in a song cycle for tenor and piano, *Fibonacci Poems* (2017).

His first novel, *Stephen Dearsley's Summer of Love* (Ward Wood Publishing, 2013) is set in Brighton in the summer of 1967. It was longlisted for the Polari Prize 2014. His second novel, *Blue Notes, Still Frames* (Ward Wood Publishing, 2016), also set in Brighton, brings together an aspiring group of photographers and musicians in the year 1994.

At Granada Television, after working in every department from politics to light entertainment, he became a producer-director of arts documentaries and then Executive Producer, Music and Arts. He made arts programmes for ITV, BBC, Channel Four, and for broadcasters in the US (WNET and Disney), in Japan (NHK) and Germany (WDR). His television credits include *Celebration, God Bless America, My Generation, Menuhin's Children* and *It Was Twenty Years Ago Today*.